SELF-GUIDE TO DEI

UNDERSTANDING DIVERSITY, EQUITY AND INCLUSION AT THE WORKPLACE

SU JOUN

This book is dedicated to

MJ and SJ
and
D@W

LET'S HAVE A CONVERSATION

Hello! I am glad you are here.

To understand diversity, equity and inclusion (DEI) at the workplace, let's have a one-on-one conservation. There are no chapters in this book - it was written to flow like a conversation between you and me. Like all good conversations, I look forward to sharing honest thoughts and reactions to better understand our own and other people's work experiences.

Let's turn the page to start the conversation.

What you see and feel at work may not be what others see and feel at work.

If you have a sibling, did you have the exact same experience growing up? If you don't have a sibling, think of a friend who has a sibling. Did they have the exact same experience growing up?

''_____

_____

_____

_____

_____

_____

_____

_____

_____

_____

_____

_____

_____

_____

_____ ''

At work, do you have the exact same experience as your coworkers?

"
_____

_____

_____

_____

_____

_____

_____

_____

_____

_____

_____

_____

_____

_____

_____
                                                          "

What are your thoughts about **what you see and feel at work may not be what others see and feel at work**?

"

_____

_____

_____

_____

_____

_____

_____

_____

_____

_____

_____

_____

_____

_____

_____

_____

"

Additional note:

During a training session that I was facilitating with the executives of an organization in the mid-west, we were discussing systemic barriers and challenges including bias and microaggressions that some folks experience at work.

The Chief Operating Officer of the organization raised his hand and said –

"I hear and I appreciate what you are saying. But these barriers and challenges you are speaking about, these biases and microaggressions – I cannot say that I have seen it. In my many years of working, I just haven't seen these things. And I just don't see it happening in my organization. I don't see these things happening here."

I nodded and said –

"Thank you for sharing that. It is great that you have not seen these barriers in the workplaces and organizations."

After a pause, I added -

*"I would also ask that you consider the following - **what you see and feel at work may not be what others see and feel at work.** People could work right next to each other in the same department and have different experiences at work. Even within our families, siblings have very different experiences growing up in the same household."*

He listened to me, leaned back in his chair, and gave a short nod.

Two weeks later, he volunteered to introduce our next training session with his team. In his introduction, he said -

*"In spite of what you think you know, pay attention to this session. It never occurred to me for some reason that others could have different work experiences from me even when we work at the same place. I have this quote written down and up in my office so that I don't forget - **what you see and feel at work may not be what others see and feel at work.** I look at it every day so that I remember."*

Now, I ask that you also take the time to think and reflect - and not simply assume and react - as you read through the next pages and as you respond to the questions.

"Best qualified" when hiring and promoting people may not be as objective as we think.

In your career up until now, have you always been hired, demoted, or promoted purely based on your qualifications?

"

                                                                    "

Has someone you know ever gotten a job interview because of a connection (relative, friend, previous colleague, etc.) or referral?

"

_____

_____

_____

_____

_____

_____

_____

_____

_____

_____

_____

_____

_____

_____ "

Do you think that all the candidates who applied for a job always get ranked purely based on years of relevant experience, skills and education?

"_____

_____

_____

_____

_____

_____

_____

_____

_____

_____

_____

_____

_____

_____

_____

_____ "

And do you think the one who got ranked at the very top is always the one who got hired?

"
_____

_____

_____

_____

_____

_____

_____

_____

_____

_____

_____

_____

_____

                                          "

Why do you think being **"best qualified"** could be subjective and not as objective as we think?

"

_____

_____

_____

_____

_____

_____

_____

_____

_____

_____

_____

_____

_____

_____

_____

_____ "

There was never a time when someone achieved success purely on merits alone.

Did everyone you know achieve success purely based on their merits?

"

"

How did one's connections/network, access to additional resources (like money, extra time, information, etc.), personality that matched their boss, liking the same sports team, etc. help?

"

_____

_____

_____

_____

_____

_____

_____

_____

_____

_____

_____

_____

_____

_____

"

What are your thoughts about achieving **success purely based on merits alone**?

"

                                                                           "

Instead of just telling people to "speak up" more, let's remove the barriers that are preventing them from speaking up.

Why do you think just **telling people to speak up more**
may not work?

"
_____

_____

_____

_____

_____

_____

_____

_____

_____

_____

_____

_____

_____

_____
"

In addition to possible internal reasons (introversion, lack of confidence, etc.), what **external** barriers could be preventing people from speaking up?

"

_____

_____

_____

_____

_____

_____

_____

_____

_____

_____

_____

_____

_____

"

How do you think it feels to be told to "speak up more" and yet not feel safe to do so?

"

"

Let's remember our gut feelings are often biased.

Where do you think your gut feelings (positive or negative) come from?

"_____

_____

_____

_____

_____

_____

_____

_____

_____

_____

_____

_____

_____

_____

_____

_____ "

Are gut feelings based on extensive research?

"

_____

_____

_____

_____

_____

_____

_____

_____

_____

_____

_____

_____

_____

_____

_____

_____

"

When you think about it, are other people's gut feelings about you all accurate?

"

,,

When you think about it, are your gut feelings about others all accurate?

"
_____

_____

_____

_____

_____

_____

_____

_____

_____

_____

_____

_____

_____

_____

_____
"

How often do you use your gut feelings to make decisions about people at work?

"

"

Microaggressions may be difficult to describe, but we know what it feels like.

Describe a time when you were micro-aggressed (felt slighted, snubbed, invalidated, and/or underestimated due to being of a certain identity – intentionally or unintentionally):

"_____

_____

_____

_____

_____

_____

_____

_____

_____

_____

_____

_____

_____

_____

_____

_____"

Describe a time when you micro-aggressed someone:

"
_____

_____

_____

_____

_____

_____

_____

_____

_____

_____

_____

_____

_____

_____

_____

_____
"

Why do you think microaggressions could be difficult to talk about at the workplace?

"
_____

_____

_____

_____

_____

_____

_____

_____

_____

_____

_____

_____

_____

_____
"

If we are not actively including people, we may be passively excluding them.

Share a time when you were (intentionally or unintentionally) excluded from something (a meeting, a conversation, a project, an event, a chance at an opportunity, etc.) at work.

"_____

_____

_____

_____

_____

_____

_____

_____

_____

_____

_____

_____

_____

_____"

Share a time when someone sought you out to make sure you were included. If that person had not sought you out or made sure you were included, would you have been included otherwise?

"_____

_____

_____

_____

_____

_____

_____

_____

_____

_____

_____

_____

_____

_____

_____

_____"

What do you think about **if we are not actively including people, we may be passively excluding them** at the workplace?

"_____

_____

_____

_____

_____

_____

_____

_____

_____

_____

_____

_____

_____

_____ "

It is not about the intent;
it is about the impact.

What is the difference between the **intent** vs. the **impact** of something that was said or done?

"

"

Why is **intent** important?

"

,,

Why would **impact** be more important than **intent** (when someone tells a hurtful joke, how a boss consistently "picks on" a team member, when someone is interrupted repeatedly in a meeting, and so on)?

"
_____

_____

_____

_____

_____

_____

_____

_____

_____

_____

_____

_____

_____

_____
"

Additional note:

Of course, intention matters. A lot. However, focusing only on the intention minimizes the actual impact. We assume if it wasn't intended, the impact does not exist at all. I have seen people genuinely hurt by something that was said or done, and that hurt be dismissed with a "they didn't mean anything by it".

Share a time when you were hurt by something said or done and it was dismissed with "that was not the intention":

"_____

_____

_____

_____

_____

_____

_____

_____

_____

_____

_____

_____

_____
                                            "

NOW, LET'S HEAR FROM OTHERS

Now that we have reflected on our own experiences and thoughts, let's hear directly from others. Here are a few of what people have shared with me about their negative experiences at work:

"I have been at this company for 20 years. I see others get promoted all around me, but I am still stuck at the same level for years. I got promoted twice in my first 5 years and then nothing. It is almost like I cannot go any further. I even went back to school to get a master's degree. Nothing happened. My manager tells me that I am doing great work, but not "quite leadership material yet". I have had mentors – I have followed their advice on how to get ahead. I have read many books, volunteered for things, and networked. I work hard – I hardly ever miss a day of work, I mean, I work from home even when I am sick, I always take on more work. I get along with everybody. I don't know what more I can do. I don't want to leave this company, but I may have to."

"I am stuck – I cannot win. If I speak up, I am seen as 'difficult' and 'too strong', but if I am quiet, then they assume I am just happy with how things are. What am I supposed to do?"

"Just because we are a nonprofit and do good work for the community, we think we are immune to racism. We are not. Lot of words the senior leaders use is cringe-worthy and outdated. When we give them feedback, they get super defensive."

"I am an immigrant, and English is my second language. I work really really hard – I just keep my head down and work really hard. But I feel invisible. I feel like I just keep cranking out work and they see me almost as a machine and not as a human."

"My company announced that they really want to work on diversity and inclusion. They encouraged everyone to speak up and share and that these conversations were 'safe spaces'. In one of these group discussions, I shared that I do not see any Black people in senior leadership. Many others agreed with me and said that something needs to be done to have more representation in senior leadership. The next day, I found out that someone in the group discussion told HR said that my comment made them feel attacked. These conversations and group discussions just stopped after that with no explanation. So much for 'safe spaces'."

"I feel like I never left high school. There are so many cliques. They go to lunch together. They dress alike. They talk about the dinners that their families have had together, about the trips they have been on together and laugh at something that happened. They have private jokes. Here is the thing: they are not mean to me – they say HI, they smile and ask me how my weekend was. They just don't really include me."

"Sometimes, I can just scream. I tell people at work that there is bias in promotions and microaggressions are happening every day - they sort of just not respond. So I keep bringing these things up until people acknowledge what I am saying. One day, my manager pulled me aside and told me that maybe I should take a break from 'keep bringing up only the problems'. He said, 'It is not all bad here, right? I mean we do some things right, right?' I did not really know how to respond to that."

"Everyone on my team loves walking meetings, but I have a bad back. Not sure how to say something."

"I get interrupted in meetings all the time. They either pepper me with questions or share their thoughts and I never get to finish even one sentence."

"I went to HR [Human Resources] at my work with some issues that I was having with my boss. Well, I will never do that again, the process that I had to go through to file a complaint was a nightmare, and I had a feeling that they told my boss about my complaint. It was so uncomfortable. I don't think HR is on my side."

"Unless you are friends with the boss, you really aren't going to get ahead."

Which of these experiences is like something you have experienced?

"_____

_____

_____

_____

_____

_____

_____

_____

_____

_____

_____

_____

_____

_____

_____ "

Do you think it is entirely an individual's fault for their negative experience at work? In other words, did they bring it upon themselves?

"

_____

_____

_____

_____

_____

_____

_____

_____

_____

_____

_____

_____

_____

_____
                                              ""

While these are examples of negative experiences, many people have positive experiences at work. Do you think they realize that others may not be having the same positive experience? If so, would they blame the individuals for their negative experiences ("they are not hard workers", "they have a bad attitude", or "they don't hustle like I do")?

"
_____

_____

_____

_____

_____

_____

_____

_____

_____

_____

_____

_____

_____

_____
"

Actions, to be more inclusive, do not have to be big - small actions can make big impact.

SMALL ACTIONS FOR BIG IMPACT

We assume we must make big changes to make big impact. It is often the small changes that can make the biggest impact. Small actions and behaviors are what make up an organization's culture. What people experience, see, hear, and feel daily is the culture of the organization. Many small actions can move the needle, cause a shift, make a meaningful change, and even create a revolution.

Here are some things we can all do:

✓ Work to get people's names (nicknames, pronunciation, spelling, etc.) and other identifiers that they shared, such as their preferred pronouns and their family status, correct. If you get it wrong, ask for the correction, apologize, and get it right the next time.

✓ Allow for silence after asking a question. For some of us, it takes a few minutes to gather our thoughts, to formulate our thoughts into words, and/or to access the risk of sharing them. Giving 20-30 seconds of silences allows enough "airtime space" for more to speak up.

✓ Instead of telling people "to speak up more" ask them what barriers can be removed that is preventing them from speaking up, and work to remove those barriers one by one.

✓ Listen fully and believe people's experiences. Assume most folks do not lie. Listen and show interest in their stories by hearing them out, without interruption, and without picking apart what they said or how they said it.

✓ Amplify someone every day. If you notice someone say something or write something, but no one is paying attention to it, then amplify them by saying or writing like –

> "Fatima made a good point earlier."

> "As Alex mentioned, it is important to note that…"

> "Derek had a good idea that I would like to hear more about."

Notice we are not speaking for folks, forcing them to speak, or even agreeing with them. Amplifying is simply increasing the chance that when people say or write something, it is acknowledged.

✓ At a minimum, raise the question. Ask if the signs posted in the break room can be read by everyone or if they should be in a bigger font size. Ask if the company picnic has food that everyone can eat and enjoy. Ask if the event venue has single stall restrooms or all gender restrooms. Ask what barriers could exist that may prevent someone from being able to utilize the resources, information, tools, or facilities.

✓ And when possible, assume there is a need and make the accommodation. Offer instructions in different languages, in larger font size, and in audio. Have all gender bathrooms, changing rooms, and dress codes. Have different dietary options. Have the team get-together event during office hours in case folks have to pick up kids from daycare. Have meeting rooms that can be easily accessed and utilized by people with all physical abilities.

We all want and need different things for us to feel included and comfortable. When our needs are met and we feel comfortable, that is when we feel like we belong.

Which of these "small acts" will you do? (Better to do 2 or
3 consistently than to start doing them all only to fizz out
later).

"
_____

_____

_____

_____

_____

_____

_____

_____

_____

_____

_____

_____

_____

_____

_____
                                                     "

What "small acts" can you encourage others to do?

"
_____

_____

_____

_____

_____

_____

_____

_____

_____

_____

_____

_____

_____

_____

_____
                                              "

WHAT'S NEXT

It was good to "talk" with you. Thank you for having this conversation with me about bias, microaggressions, meritocracy, assumptions, and people's experiences at work. Hope you were able to take the time to think, reflect, and gain some additional perspective.

You may have noticed that while this book is titled **Self Guide to Diversity, Equity and Inclusion* (DEI)**, we have not directly talked about diversity, equity and inclusion. In essence, everything we discussed in this book is about DEI. DEI work is not an abstract or a political topic. It is recognizing and acknowledging that there isn't always fairness for everyone at work and that there are things that can be done to increase fairness so that more can feel comfortable, can fully contribute, and be successful at work.

And this conversation and work do not end here. Let's continue the journey by:

✓ Continuing to think and reflect through the statements and other parts of this book.

- ✓ What do you agree with? What do you disagree with?

- ✓ Reflecting on your responses – what defensiveness did you notice kicking in?

- ✓ Sharing some of these statements with others and seeking their reflections and responses.

- ✓ Role modeling one or more of the "small acts" publicly and consistently inspiring others to follow.

- ✓ Following through on the commitments you make on the next page.

Let's work together to make the workplace (and outside of the workplace) fairer for us and for others.

*Diversity literally means "variety, a mix".

*Equity means the "quality of being fair and impartial".

*Inclusion means "the action of being included within a group".

How will you continue your journey? List your **commitments** here:

►_____

_____

_____

_____

_____

_____

►_____

_____

_____

_____

_____

►_____

_____

_____

_____

_____

Come back in a few months after implementing your commitments. How did they work out?

▶_____

_____

_____

_____

_____

_____

▶_____

_____

_____

_____

_____

_____

▶_____

_____

_____

_____

_____

What will you do differently?

►_____

_____

_____

_____

_____

_____

_____

►_____

_____

_____

_____

_____

_____

►_____

_____

_____

_____

_____

_____

What commitments will you keep doing? What new commitments will you do?

► _____

_____

_____

_____

_____

_____

_____

► _____

_____

_____

_____

_____

_____

► _____

_____

_____

_____

_____

**"The world is changed
by your example,
not by your opinion."**

-Paulo Coelho

www.ingramcontent.com/pod-product-compliance
Lightning Source LLC
Chambersburg PA
CBHW071122210326
41519CB00020B/6385